QUEEN ZANTU

THE ATTACK
AGAINST FAIRYVILLE

D1509662

To: Brechton Park Library
Readers!

8/12/16

Enjoy my thoughts & ideas

Tabitha Jef
aka Mrs. Spirit

TABLE OF CONTENTS

QUEEN ZANTU
THE ATTACK AGAINST FAIRYVILLE
Written by Tabitha Fefee
Copyright 2016 @ by Tabitha Fefee

CHAPTER ONE
ZANTU GOES TO FAIRYVILLE

Zantu is a shy, seven years old girl in second grade. She and her parents live so far away from family that she often felt lonely and sad. Zantu's father is an officer in the military and this causes them to have to move a lot. Always having to move was so hard on Zantu. Whenever she made new friends, it was time to move again.

Zantu is very angry at her parents for moving so much. She would tell them that she hated her life and that she was lonely. Because she doesn't have any friends, she comes home from school, locks herself in her room and just cries. Being the only child and not having friends is so unfair she would think. She asked her father if he could get a new job so that they would not have to move so much. She just wanted friends. She felt if she only had a brother, a sister or even a puppy to play with, her life would be wonderful. They said maybe later, but not now. It just wasn't a good time they told her. Zantu said "you're the worst parents ever and I hate you." She ran to her room crying. She would walk around the house looking sad trying to change their minds. She made up imaginary friends just to have someone to play with.

One day while Zantu was playing, something strange happened. The window was opened and a beautiful little fairy flew into her room. Her wings were pink, her hair was orange and she sparkled as she flew around the room. Zantu was so startled that she screamed as she peaked from under her bed. "Who are you?" "Where did you come from?" Zantu shook her head, because she thought she must be imagining things. Her friends were imaginary, after all. I'm Selena and I'm from Fairyville an enchanted world of wonder. I'm looking for someone to play with and be friends. Will you be my friend? Would you like to see a magical and enchanted place? Sure ugh... I guess.

In order for Zantu to enter Fairyville, she had to be fairy size, so Selena waved her magic fairy wand and sprinkled fairy dust all over her. Zantu was so amazed and excited because she was now a fairy with beautiful fairy wings to fly.

Fairyville was wonderful. She made friends with all the other fairies and they loved her. She never wanted to leave this enchanted and exciting new world. The village was bright, with little houses where everyone played and visited each other. They were always happy, never sad. They were never lonely. She spent the day playing, flying and having fun. She had lots of friends. Before she knew it, dusk was drawing near and Zantu had to leave to go back home. Selena changed her back to her original size.

Back home, Zantu didn't sleep at all thinking about the magical world and when she could go back. The excitement was too much to bare. She couldn't focus when she was in school and would daydream about the fun she had while at Fairyville. Selena would visit Zantu every day, sprinkle her with fairy dust and off they would go back to Fairyville for more fun and adventure.

Zantu parent's tried to encourage her to go out to play with the children in the neighborhood. They felt she was spending too much time in her room. Little did they know, she was visiting her friends in Fairyville. One day when Zantu came home from school, her parents told her they had to move again.   This was very upsetting news to Zantu. She didn't know what to do. She cried...” mom, dad I don't want to leave. Please can't we stay?” Zantu ran to her room and called out to her friend Selena. Selena where are you? Please come I need you. I want to change into a fairy forever. I never want to go back home!

Selena heard Zantu and came to help her new friend. She sprinkled Zantu with fairy dust and off they went to Fairyville. I will never have to move again thought Zantu. When the other fairies found out Zantu had returned, they were very excited. They loved Zantu and thought of her as one of them. Little did she know, she was one of their own as it was her destiny to reign as queen of Fairyville.

CHAPTER TWO
ZANTU DISCOVERS HER LEGACY

Although Fairyville was a happy place where fairies played and enjoyed each other, there was a mean witch fairy who did not want Zantu to take her rightful place on the throne. So, she plotted, captured Zantu and locked her away in a cage.

Zantu cried and asked to go home. The witch said you will stay in Fairyville locked in this cage forever. The witch didn't want Zantu to reign on her throne and instill new orders and decrees. The witch had control over Fairyville without a queen being in charge. Zantu asked Selena to go home and get her parents. Selena would have to use the child like heart dust to change them into kids so they could enter Fairyville and believe.

Selena was captured and thrown into the cage with Zantu. Zantu cried and said "I just wanted friends to play with, I never really wanted to stay here forever. Please help me get out."

The fairies worked together when the witch and her servants went to sleep. It took twenty of the fairies to unlock the cage with the big key before they could free them.

Selena said Zantu I have something to tell you. I came to your room and changed you into a fairy for a reason. You are the queen of Fairyville. What? That's couldn't be true exclaimed Zantu. "How is this possible?" Selena explained that many years ago a human boy and a fairy fell in love. The young fairy asked the fairy king and queen to change her into a human forever, they married and had children. You're part of that heritage. The throne rights are given to the 10th generation and that's you.

Selena showed Zantu her throne and her robe of majesty with the plans wrapped in a scroll. We hoped your information would be safe in the scroll under the past queen's protection. When the last queen was dethroned the information went public and your secret was no longer safe. Your address and name was uncovered and fairies could come looking for their future queen. So I came looking for my future queen, it was an honor to meet you and play with the next queen of the fairies. Ask your parents they know all about the story

Zantu's mother said we made a decision and daddy joined the military to travel and to keep you safe as long as we could sweetheart. We just wanted to protect your childhood. Please don't be angry you'll understand when you have kids of your own someday. Zantu's parents said we hope you understand and forgive us. We love you honey. Sorry future queen.

Zantu was very angry that her parents did not tell her the truth. Selena said you must make up your own mind to be Queen of the fairies. This is not a decision your parents can make for you. This decision must come from you alone.

Zantu and the fairies fought dragons and captured mean fairies that were their enemies. They were bad for the Fairyville world. Queen Zantu was brave and unafraid. Zantu reign on the throne for six months and was having fun. She could also use her magic wand to see her parents. Zantu's parents looked for her everywhere and they even called the police. They were scared and afraid that they would never see her again. Zantu could see her parents crying. She said "I must leave and go back home to be with them." Selena said "you can't ever go." Queen Zantu said I order you to allow me to leave. Never will you leave said Selena.

Zantu had to reign on the throne for a year before she could pass the throne over to someone else. Selena was mean and had reasons for wanting Zantu to stay in Fairyville; she was her second in command. She never went to get her parents, because she never wanted Zantu to leave. Zantu had to stay in charge for a year and then turn over the throne to her.

Selena pointed out to Zantu how lonely and bored she was in the human world. She said you hated your parents for making you move so often and you didn't have any friends. I gave you a whole new world and you want to leave? I can't allow that to happen.

Queen Zantu had to fight for her throne rights. Another fairy name Bella went home to get Zantu's parents to help change Selena's mind and get Zantu back home with them. Bella had to change them into fairies to enter the magic world. Queen Zantu's Parents said please allow her to come home and be with us, we love her and miss her dearly. Things will change for Queen Zantu. Daddy's job will not move him again for years and we can be a family again. Queen Zantu's Parents said hold on to her throne, wand and robe until she's an adult and she can come back if she wishes.

A Queen's responsibility and duties are reading letters from the public, official papers and briefing notes; audiences with political ministers or ambassadors; and meetings with her private secretaries to discuss daily business and her future plans. The Queen undertakes constitutional and representational duties which have developed over one thousand years.

Queen Zantu wore the belt of truth that helped her stay focused and be truthful. She also had on the breast plate of righteousness that helped her maintain the quality of being morally right or justifiable. She always had her feet fitted with readiness and ready for every battle that came her way. She always wore the helmet of salvation that shielded her from life's hard hits. She kept the sword of the spirit in her heart at all times and stayed spiritually led by God during her battles of life. She always had the shield of faith next to her bed and next to her heart.

Queen Zantu had to display nine character virtues in order to maintain her kingdom rights successfully. The fruit of the Spirit: love, joy, peace, patience, kindness, goodness, faithfulness, gentleness and self-control. When the Queen achieved these virtues throughout her kingdom she would receive nine metals of bravery and spiritual healing. She would obtain these virtues only through prayer and fasting. She had every fairy throughout the kingdom to fast and pray with her. When Queen Zantu had a lot of difficult times in her kingdom, she remembered that suffering produces perseverance; perseverance produces character, character produces hope and hope does not disappoint. The town would pour out their hearts to her and her kingdom. Queen Zantu learned that spiritual characteristics are produced by the Holy Spirit.

Queen Zantu spoke and said my place is with my family and I will come back and take my place again as Queen, when I'm an adult. She was happy to be back home with her family. The Queen made a decree that fairies can make up their own minds and live their own lives and not be captured by the witch again.

Zantu told her family about the great adventures she had in Fairyville and all the fun she had as a fairy. She made lots of friends at her school and in the neighborhood and enjoyed spending time with them. She learned how to be brave and make new friends from being in Fairyville and taking risk to share her heart with others. She became the most popular person in her school. Life was good and happy.

Queen Zantu would go back to Fairyville from time to time and sit on her throne and instill orders and decrees and make sure Fairyville was being run correctly.

Selena was the Queen whenever Queen Zantu wasn't available. The witch of the fairies was in jail for locking up the Queen Zantu. Things in Fairyville were going very well.

Every year in Fairyville they had summer and winter games against each other to win a gold trophy and become healthy. The games were made up of two teams. The two teams were 2000 fairies on each team with a coach leading the games. Fairies from other villages came to watch the games. The games brought out the best in everybody and they had a festival throughout the entire season. The fairies prepared for the games all year around. Queen Zantu would charge admission to enter the gymnasiums and watch the games and enjoy the festivities. The gymnasiums held 8000 fairies and friends. The parade was beautifully designed and the food was delicious. The fairies sprinkled dust on all the animals making them fly and they were also in charge of entertainment for the games. They had a puppet show and performed magic tricks to entertain the crowds.

The town was happy and glowing with excitement. There was a big parade, balloons, dancers and singers throughout the streets of Fairyville during these fun times. The games brought the fairies together for the better. During the festivities there was a man walking on stilts and another guy doing fire tricks. Summer games lasted from March through August. The summer games were volleyball, soccer and swimming. The winter games lasted September through February. The winter games were made up of skiing, sledding and tubing.

Queen Selena canceled all the games. Fairyville were in an uproar about this decision. She stopped the games to control the fairies. She didn't want anything that Queen Zantu set up to keep happening in her kingdom. Queen Selena was very mean and unkind. Selena wanted the fairies to walk in fear and always be afraid.

The fairies would not challenge her decision because, they did not want to be punished. Fairyville lost a lot of money and support by canceling the games. Selena did not care that the games brought the fairies together and drew them closer to one another.

Queen Zantu would give food out to the poor fairies in other villages with the money that was collected throughout the gaming seasons. Fairyville was known for helping others to survive.

The games were set up for the fairies to focus on others and work together as a team. They were unified and fought together in battle because of the games. Fairyville was unstoppable when they had games. Without the games they were vulnerable in battle because the games helped them sharpen their battle skills. They could not be defeated because of the games and the lessons that they learned. Queen Selena wanted to break the fairies spirit and keep them under her control. That's just what she did. Fairyville wasn't the same and something had to change.

CHAPTER THREE
THE BATTLE TO SAVE FAIRYVILLE

Something urgent happened in Fairyville the 4000 fairies were under attack by the mush trolls and were being defeated. Queen Zantu's presence was needed at once. On Queen Zantu's eighteenth birthday it was time for her to take her rightful place as Queen. She ordered the fairies to rally together and sent her best fairies to battle. The fairies put on their helmets, shields and took their sword and set up on the front line for attack against the mush trolls. Queen Zantu asked the King of the toads to come and help with the fight but, he refused because Selena had made a mess of the kingdom.

Queen Zantu had lost alliance with everyone who had helped Fairyville in battle before. They now refused to help because Selena had made enemies with all of them.

He was furious and said Selena stopped giving us gold and silver to protect the fairies. She said our services were no longer needed in her kingdom. Queen Zantu was very angry and had a lot of orders and decrees to change.

The Mush trolls were ugly and sneaky and they sat in the garden of the fields rolled up and ready for attack. The trolls heard that Selena wasn't the true Queen in charge and it was time for battle, because the kingdom were vulnerable. The trolls were waiting for the right time to attack the fairies. Only the true Queen could decree an order to start a fight for battle. The trolls defeated 50 fairies and it was time to go to war.

Queen Zantu ordered the fairy army to shoot the cannons in battle if needed. The trolls also knew that if the true Queen wasn't running the throne it was a violation of the law. The trolls knew the law very well because, they protected the fairies for years against their enemies. She said let them find their own food we have better things to do in my kingdom than to feed a bunch of trolls.

Selena did not want to follow Zantu's orders and decrees that she had left in place for the fairies' protections. Selena wanted to run the kingdom the way she saw fit. The fairies weren't listening to Selena's orders anymore and they sent word to Queen Zantu because, fairies were being defeated under Selena's orders. She never wanted Zantu to return back to Fairyville and take back her throne.

Selena had been the Queen for 11 years and the fairies was scared to challenge her authority or they would be killed. Bella was Selena's second in command. Bella feared for her life everyday being under Selena's command. Selena became selfish and unkind. Bella thought, Selena was my true friend before she was appointed queen.

Selena hired someone to kill Queen Zantu she didn't want to give her throne rights back. Queen Zantu would walk through the battlefield line to make sure the fight was safe. Selena would have her put to death on the front line as she walked through. Bella wanted to send a letter to alert Zantu but, Selena found out and had her beaten and flogged in front of the entire kingdom and threw her in jail. Queen Selena said; if anyone else crosses me, they will be destroyed. Let this be a lesson to all the fairies don't ever cross your queen again.

Selena instilled an order that every fairy had to give taxes to her and the kingdom.

The orders were putting a strain on the fairies. If they refused they could be thrown in jail at once.

The fairies were very frustrated with Queen Selena and they had a meeting and wanted her dethroned. Everyone in the kingdom was afraid to stand up against the Queen because of fear of being flogged or thrown in jail. The fairies followed Selena with fear and trembling. They still honored her as Queen, but they lived in fear of her. The panic struck the entire fairies and they were afraid for their lives and their families' lives as well. Queen Zantu chose Selena to lead her fairies and she was not doing a good job.

Selena had guards around her everywhere she went. She had guards around the dungeon to keep the prisoners locked up and guarded. One day a guard said Bella, I will let you out and the other fairies will help you go get Queen Zantu, this madness has to stop immediately. Five fairies helped Bella escape. They had a hide-out already and a getaway plan in place for her to alert Queen Zantu.

Bella reached Queen Zantu and told her that Fairyville was under attack and she needed to take her place as Queen. She also informed her that fairies were being defeated on the battle field by mush trolls. Selena wouldn't give up her throne that easily. Selena had arranged someone to kill Queen Zantu's parents. She was furious.

Queen Zantu hid her parents deep inside a cave and had guards protecting them. She ordered them to stay close to her parents and guard them with their lives. She had stationed guards around herself as well. She sent word for Selena to come meet her face to face and sit down and talk. She told Zantu I have served as Queen for 11 years while you lived a very comfortable life with your family. Selena said this is not over watch your back.

The mush trolls looked like mushrooms sitting in the garden and it's hard to see them coming. The trolls became very anger and lurked around the kingdom listening at night and started attacking any fairies they saw away from the kingdom. The trolls found a way to release the witch from the dungeon and they served and protected her kingdom. The witch tried using her magic spell book to capture the fairies and make them work and serve her. The trolls and the witch joined forces and fought against the fairies. All day long the battle raged. Queen Zantu was propped in a chariot and heavily guarded as she oversaw the battle against the mush trolls.

The plan was to overthrow Fairyville. Queen Zantu heard about the plan and sent for the King of the toads to help them fight the trolls and the witch. Selena made a mess of things in Fairyville.

CHAPTER FOUR
EVERYONE REFUSES TO HELP THE FAIRIES

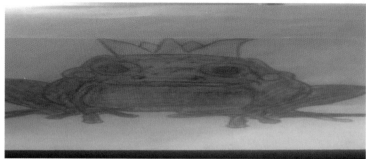

Queen Zantu had to clean up Selena's mess and get the kingdom back in order. She would give gold and silver to the king of the toads. They would work together and fight off other predators and animals that wanted to eat the fairies. Selena refused to meet with the king of the toads and give them gold and silver for their protection. She told the King of the toads the fairies didn't need their protection any longer. He said the gold and silver helps us buy food. Selena said leave my kingdom. She was making enemies with the animals that protected Fairyville.

Queen Zantu sent word for the king of the beavers to come and help them fight but, he refused. Everyone was aware that Selena was not the true Queen of the fairies and they were furious. So all the decrees and orders that was in place were void with other animals for the fairies' protection.

Queen Zantu found out quickly that she didn't have any help with the battle. 200 fairies were killed in battle. The trolls were defeating them. They were killing the fairies in their sleep as well. She requested the king of the trolls to come and speak with her and work something out. He said you and Queen Selena lied to me and tricked us all. The law states there is no going back and we must fight it out in battle. He said I will kill every fairy in Fairyville.

Queen Zantu said I will have your head on a silver platter. The king of the troll said we will see, Queen Zantu you should give up. We have defeated 200 fairies and will kill you all before this battle is over. You are defeated. Queen Zantu said never.

The queen had a meeting with the fairies and said we must consider it pure joy whenever we face trials of many kinds, because we know that the testing of our faith develops perseverance. We must be mature and completely prepared for this battle not lacking nothing and develop a solid plan of attack. Queen Zantu took the silver and gold found in the temple and in the treasuries of the royal palace and sent it as a gift to the king of the trolls. The king was happy to meet and talk with the Queen in private. The king of the troll said we out number you in size. I kept you safe and protected and we fought all your battles. He said you don't have anything new to defeat us with. Queen Zantu had to come up with another plan against the trolls and the witch. The trolls and the witch were too powerful for the fairies. Everyone that she had partnered with would no longer help the fairies fight. The lieutenant in charge of the battle reported to Queen Zantu that they were losing many fairies and needed some help. Queen Zantu had only one way to save her kingdom. She used the cannon fireballs against the trolls and the witch, but her efforts were unsuccessful. When the word got out that the kingdom was vulnerable, they came to take over and challenge the fairies to battle.

There was a giant name Garth on the south side of Fairyville he was 7 feet tall and weighed 400 pounds with three heads. He challenged Queen Zantu to fight in battle to take control of her kingdom. The Queen wondered why everyone who had helped Fairyville before now wanted to destroy it.

She summoned her commander in chief and asked for his help. The Queen launched the cannon fireballs against the big giant but he kept getting back up and charging toward the fairies and trying to eat them. The fairies would toss big borders and use their magic dusk, making different objects fly to hit the giant. He was so tall that the fireballs missed him every time.

Fairyville was in big trouble and something needed to change. Queen Zantu had to come up with a very successful plan to save Fairyville. This was the first time Zantu was scared and afraid for her kingdom.

The fairies would stand on a big ladder and try to defeat the giant but, nothing worked. The giant yelled I will come back tomorrow and give you another chance to try to defeat me. The queen went to her room and cried because, it looked hopeless and impossible.

She sent word for King Asmar to come before her throne and have dinner with her and talk. King Asmar was mean, callous and thought only of himself. King Asmar commander of the army, a great solider and was known throughout Fairyville. Every fairy girl in Fairyville wanted to marry King Asmar. She had to marry a king of the fairies in a new town to double their size. He said I will marry you and take control over your kingdom and you must bow down before me and worship me. He said a woman should be seen and not heard. You will only speak when spoken too. Your throne will be mine and I will do with it what I see fit. King Asmar said I have my own staff, I don't need your staff's help. I will fire your people and start over. He said I will take your gold and silver and only give you what you need to live on and to maintain Fairyville.

A servant girl said Queen may I speak with you in private, you can't accept his offer. The Queen said I have no other choice, I must save the kingdom. The Queen was angry and said servant girl leave me at once before I put you in jail. The Queen was under a lot

of pressure. She said I just wanted to grow up and not have so much pressure in my life.

Maybe I can give up my throne and things can go back to the way it used to be. Zantu said

I don't want to be the Queen any longer. This is too much for one person. I just got

accepted to college and is time for me to live my life. I'm only 18 years old and I'm tired

but, the fairies are counting on me. Zantu said I must stay focused on my task. I must not

make everything about me and what I want out of life. She said I wanted to go to college,

get married, live in a big house and travel. Zantu said running a kingdom is too hard.

Selena how did you manage? Selena said one day at a time.

Zantu thought to herself, I don't want this responsibility any longer. Selena said you

were born for such a time as this. Selena said I was born a fairy so I'm use to this life. You

were born to be the queen you think of others and consider them first. I'm very selfish and

I made a mess of things in Fairyville. Selena said I let the kingdom power go to my head.

I became very arrogant. I hope the fairies can find it in their hearts to forgive me and my

bad behavior. My Queen give it some time and you will get use to running the kingdom

and making decision for everybody. You have always put the fairies first in every decision

that was made for the kingdom. That's why you're the true Queen. Selena said trust that

the decisions that you make are the correct ones for the fairies and the kingdom. Selena

said you're not wrong for wanting those things out of life, you were human until six

months ago. Selena you are a good friend Queen Zantu said.

After deep thought she refused King Asmar's offer to marry. Zantu had to come up

with another plan to defeat the trolls and the witch. The battle lasted for months and she

had lost 400 fairies in the fight. She sent word for her second in command Henry to bring

her parents to Fairyville. He had to use the magic dusk and change them into fairies before they could enter Fairyville. They arrived in the royal carriage.

Queen Zantu needed some help, when her parents arrived she asked them what she should do. She also told them she was scared and afraid for her kingdom. Her Parents said everyone is counting on you and they told her to cast all her cares and worries upon the Lord and He'll care for you. They also told her we raised you to trust in God, so stop trying to fight this battle and let God be God in your life. Her father said honey you know what needs to be done. Zantu's parents stayed in Fairyville and guided her about important decisions. They helped her to run a successful kingdom. They talked and advised her about who she should partner with to protect her kingdom. They became her second in command. Together they came up with a peace treaty, so nothing like this would ever happen again in Fairyville.

CHAPTER FIVE
QUEEN ZANTU SEEKING GOD'S DIRECTION FOR FAIRYVILLE

She remembered everything happens for a reason and a season. She thought to herself, Selena wasn't Queen I am and she did the best that she could to run the kingdom. Zantu had to remember how much it takes to run a kingdom. She thought about all the pressure Selena. She released her from Jail and offered her the fattest calf and had a fest and apologized to Selena and thanked her. Zantu was a child and could not run a kingdom on her own and everything happens for a reason. Queen Zantu gave Selena her ring back and reached out the scepter and Selena became a close confidant to the Queen.

Queen Zantu had forgotten about the spiritual attributes that helped run a successful kingdom of the fairies. She thought about the suffering that she had endured and how perseverance will develop stronger character and hope and God does not disappoint. She thought to herself that God has poured out his love for me already. The spiritual attributes produces characteristics by the Holy Spirit not by mere discipline. Queen Zantu had a dream that the battle was worn and the trolls and the witch and the giant was defeated. The Queen had confirmation and was ready for battle. It was time to trust and rely on the true King.

Queen Zantu had to put on her full armor of God and let Him fight her battle. She had to be strong in the Lord and his mighty hand. The day of evil was here and she had to stand firm and let God be God. She had the belt of truth around her waist. She put the breast plate of righteousness on her chest and prepared for battle. She had her feet fitted with the readiness that comes from reading her bible and she had peace from within. Her faith was increasing and she placed her shield on her back and begin to speak faith to all the fairies throughout the kingdom. She placed her helmet on her head and had the sword of the spirit in her hand.

I'm going too fast and pray to God because only He can save us. We will fast and pray with a heart and a spirit focusing on God Almighty Zantu said. We'll pray until we receive a change and get wisdom and understanding and direction from God. We will praise and worship God until a change takes place. We will cry out to the God that will save us in the midst of the storm. She told Selena to have everyone in her kingdom to pray and fast for protection. She prayed and fasted for God's help in battle.

Queen Zantu said to the trolls, the witch and Garth the giant, this day the Lord will hand you over to me and we will strike you down. The Lord will give you all into our hands. We are no longer afraid. The day of evil was here and she stood firm and let God be God. Queen Zantu and the fairies were prepared, alert and ready for battle. She said we will not be defeated. She said I'm not afraid and God will deliver us. Queen Zantu asked "who's with me in this battle?" All the fairies in the kingdom said " we are my queen."

Queen Zantu said the spirit of the Lord will come upon us with power and we will be different fairies with increased faith. She said we must love the Lord our God with all our hearts and with all our souls and with all our strength.

Queen Zantu said we must trust and rely on the Lord in every situation. We must cast our cares and worries upon him and He'll see us through. She said God has never failed us and he never will. The Lord is our refuge for the oppressed. He's our stronghold in times of trouble. We're in trouble now and Lord we need your help.

Queen Zantu had forgotten that she was in a covenant relationship with God. Her enemies became God's enemies. Her kingdom became victorious, prosperous and wealthy. Fairyville was unstoppable. They won every battle that they fought. Queen Zantu put on her armor and wore a bronze helmet on her head. She had on her tunic for victory.

Garth the giant won 15 battles until now. God can make the impossible situation possible. Queen Zantu said I come against you all in the name of the Lord Almighty. The giant was finally defeated. When Queen Zantu and the fairies surrendered to God they won every battle that they faced. They trusted and relied on the Lord and He blessed her kingdom. She learned that the only person on her side that could fight and defeat her battles was the Lord Almighty. She had to learn that the hard way. She lost 400 fairies because, she was very stubborn and did not trust and rely on God and cry out for His help. She wished she could have saved their lives. She prayed for their families and sent them gold and silver. God had blessed them with so much gold and silver throughout her kingdom. Queen Zantu had the families of the dead fairies to eat and drink with her and her kingdom. She wanted to honor their lives and their fight in battle. She wanted to thank them for their sacrifice.

There was no one like her among all the Queens. She held fast to the Lord's commands and did not stop following his decrees. Queen Zantu was successful in whatever she undertook and reigned victorious on the throne for 30 years. She married a King of the fairies in the town of Bush Gardenville and they had three children. She wrote down her successful victories and her battle plans. Zantu recorded her orders and decrees for the next queen that would reign on the throne. Trust and rely on God Almighty.

Fairyville had always been run by females and she had given birth to three daughters.

The oldest girl would be queen and she could refused the throne and give it to her other sisters. Queen Zantu said it is time to pass on my throne rights to the next in line. Queen Zantu's daughters were named Zelda, Zoe and Zena. Queen Zantu said I have reigned on the throne long enough. The sisters had a big decision to make.

Who would take over the throne rights? Which sister would reign on the throne in Fairyville?

Made in the USA
Charleston, SC
18 July 2016